Vintage
CARDBOARD
CRAFTING

HANDMAKING 15 EMBELLISHED CONTAINERS

Anne Lardy

SCHIFFER
PUBLISHING

4880 Lower Valley Road • Atglen, PA 19310

CONTENTS

[Foreword]

Let me take you on a journey through time. I had great fun reproducing a few antique boxes—the kind you might come across in your grandparents' attic or a secondhand store—using fabric, Skivertex, craft papers, and decorations found at garage sales and in flea markets. You may even be able to find antique engravings that can be transfered onto fabric (see the monogram box, the 1920s box, and the watch box).

You can also make your own engravings to transfer onto fabric.

In the technique section you will learn how to make a rectangular box with a hinged lid, and another box with a fitted lid. When in doubt about any of the steps, don't hesitate to consult the Advice chapter.

Anne Lardy

[Materials and supplies]

MATERIALS

– Cutting board
– Box cutter with interchangeable blades
– Heavy slide rule
– 50 cm slide rule
– Paper knife
– Square
– Scissors
– Different-sized paste brushes (12, 25, 40 cm, for example)
– Mechanical pencil
– Compass
– Sanding block
– Polishing pad
– Gimlet and a screwdriver
– Weights and clips
– Rags
– Magazines and newspapers for pasting

SUPPLIES

Cardboard: Most of the time I use gray cardboard 2 mm thick, which is perfect for small- and medium-sized boxes. I'll tell you when I use thicker cardboard.

Cards: Thin cardstock (250 g) for the interior of the boxes. For everything that is rounded, 0.7 mm card or framing cards are used. Be careful; this card has a direction: you should curve it to find out which direction it curves or it will "break." You can also use 1 mm thick cardboard.

Kraft paper: to cut into bands the same width as the slide rule (3 cm) or a roll of sticky Kraft (3.5 cm).

Special cardboard white glue: found online.

Book muslin: for reinforcing the hinges.

Skivertex: There is a large choice of Skivertex.

Paper: There is also a large choice of paper, and don't forget wallpaper.

Fabrics: Cotton fabrics are best because they are easy to glue.

[Techniques]

Cut out of 2 mm thick cardboard:

1 bottom: 19 × 11.4 cm
2 large sides: 19.5 × 4 cm
2 small sides: 11.4 × 3.8 cm
The large sides are glued onto the sides of the bottom, and the small sides are glued onto the bottom, which explains the 2 mm difference in size (the thickness of the cardboard).

Materials
Skivertex
Printed fabric and flecked ribbon

The rectangle box in 6 steps
Cut out two (of each) bands of Kraft the same length and width as the bottom (19.5 cm and 11.4 cm). Cut the ends at an angle and glue them so that they overlap the bottom of the box (1).

Put glue along the bottom (1.5 cm) of the back of one of the long sides and place it alongside the bottom cardboard; fold the Kraft back over it with a paper knife. Do the same for the other side (2).

Glue two bands of Kraft inside the large sides (3).

Put glue along the bottom (1.5 cm) of the back of one of the short sides and put it in place on the bottom cardboard between the two long sides; fold the Kraft back over it with the paper knife. Make two bands of Kraft for the exterior of the short side (4).

Glue bands of Kraft along the bottom of the inside of the short side and on each side, moving the box around so that you can press down with the paper knife (5).

Do the second short side in the same way (6).

1

2

3

4 & 5

6

Covering the exterior of the hinged box

Cut out a band of Skivertex or fabric 47 × 7 cm, which represents the length of 2 short sides + 1 long side + 4 cm, and in width the height of the box + 1.5 cm on each side, which are the overlaps that will be folded back.

Glue the band with the height properly centered on three sides (1 small, 1 large, 1 small), with a flap 2 cm on the back of each side. This will be used later with the lid (7).

On the underneath, cut the angles and glue the overlaps under the box (8 & 9).

On the top of the box, cut out each angle (10), remove the resulting "little arrow," and glue the overlaps inside the box (11).

Covering the interior of the hinged box

Making the hinge: cut out a band 9 cm × the width of the interior of the box: 9 × 19.1 cm. Glue it astride the back and the edge of the back of the box (12). If you are making a hinge with skivertex you won't need to double it; if the hinge is made of fabric, you'll need to glue a reinforcing piece of fabric.

If you have a higher box, you can plan a hinge that returns 4 cm inside and redo a card for the inside back afterwards; it will be neater.

Interior cards: we use 250 g cardstock, which can be replaced by thin Bristol or Canson paper or any other thin paper. I haven't put the cards' measurements because they are calculated as indicated further on, but you should try them before covering them, and you should also take the thickness of the fabric or skivertex into account.

Calculating a card: width of the inside of the box – 1 mm × height of the interior – 2 mm, so for the front interior card: 19 × 3.6 cm. Cover the card with fabric, with overlaps of 1.5 cm all around. Cut the angles shown

in red in Diagram 1, fold back the top flap and glue the card onto the front interior. Glue the other overlaps onto the base of the box and the short sides (13).

Calculate the short sides' interior pieces (11.1 × 3.6

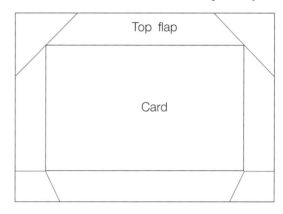

Diagram 1

cm), cover them, cut the angles shown in red in Diagram 1, fold back the top flap and the two short sides, and glue them in place inside the box (14).

Calculate the piece for the bottom of the box: length of the box – 2 mm × the interior width – 2 mm: 18.7 × 11 cm, cover it, fold back the overlaps, and glue it inside the box.

Lid

The lid of a box is calculated just as the inside pieces are. Take the exterior measurements of the box and add 4 mm onto the length and 2 mm onto the width (the lid overlaps slightly on 3 sides and is flush against the back).

So for your box: cut 250 × 12 cm out of the 2 mm thick cardboard. Cover the lid, allowing for an overlap of 1.5 cm on 3 sides and 6 cm at the back (the height of the box + 2 cm). Cut the two front angles at 2 mm from the cardboard; you can use a small corner gauge

7

8 & 9

10 & 11

12

13 & 14

that is really practical for this (you can find them in online stores).

On the back you will have to cut out a particular shape shown in red in Diagram 2 to cover the back angles correctly. Cut out along the red lines and glue the two tongues sideways to protect the angles on the hinge side (15). Glue the front flap and the 2 short sides.

For my box, I intensified the work a little by including an image on the lid. For this you cut out a card the same size as the lid and cut a hole in it (2 cm in this case). Stick this piece onto the center of the skivertex and glue the 4 overlaps under the card (16).

Center the image properly, glue it to the cardboard, and glue the piece to the cardboard. Return to Diagram 2 for the continuation.

Assembling the lid onto the box
We start by gluing the exterior hinge, and then the interior hinge. For the exterior hinge place the lid right side down on the table, place the box over it, aligning the back, and glue the hinge, pulling it tight. Leave it to completely dry out before opening the box (17).

Make a piece for the underside of the box (length – 2 mm × width – 2 mm): 19.4 × 11.6 cm, cover it, fold the overlaps underneath, and glue it to the underside of the box (18).

Glue the interior hinge, pulling it tight (19).

Calculate the measurements of a card for the underside of the lid. It's better for it to fit inside the box so that it doesn't interfere when you shut the box, so in this case you'll cut out 18.8 × 11.2 cm. Cover it, fold under the 4 overlaps and glue it to the underside of the lid.

This is an ideal box for 3 small bars of soap or for storing letters.

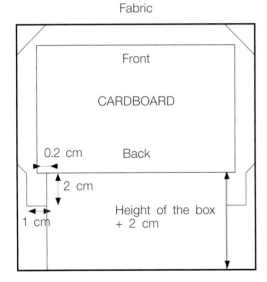

Fabric

Front

CARDBOARD

0.2 cm   Back

2 cm

1 cm   Height of the box + 2 cm

Diagram 2

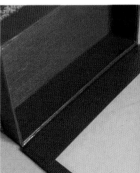

15   16   17   18   19

MAKING AND COVERING A BOX WITH A FITTED LID

Cut out of 2 mm thick cardboard:
1 bottom: 19.8 × 13.3 cm
2 large sides: 19.8 × 6 cm
2 small sides: 13.3 × 5.8 cm

Lid (to be checked after covering the box)
1 bottom: 20.5 × 14 cm
2 large sides: 20.5 × 2 cm
2 small sides: 14 × 1.8 cm

Materials
– Skivertex (available online)
– Printed fabric picked up in dressmakers' flea markets.

Making the box
Follow the 6 steps for the rectangular box.

Covering the box
The 4 sides of the box are covered. For this, cut out a band 70 × 9 cm which represents the box's perimeter (verify) + 2 cm x the height of the box + 1.5 cm overlap on the top and 1.5 cm overlap on the bottom. Glue this band all around the box: start by gluing one side at 1.5 cm from the edge and centered heightwise [1].

Next, glue the 2 other sides. Before gluing the last side, fold over the first flap and then glue the last side over it [2].

Cut away any surplus material. Fold the overlaps on the bottom and the top (see photos 8, 9 & 10 of the hinged box).

Calculate the piece for the exterior bottom (length – 2 mm × width – 2 mm): 19.8 × x 13.6 cm; cover it, fold back the overlaps, and glue it under the box. Or, as I did, cut a base out of the cardboard that overlaps the box slightly: 20.5 × 14.4 cm (the dimension of the finished lid). Cover it and glue it to the bottom of the box.

For the interior, make pieces in the same way as you did for the hinged box (see photos 13 & 14 of the hinged box). Do 2 parallel sides (the 2 large sides for example), calculate the cards (length – 1 mm × height – 2 mm): 19.3 × 5.6 cm (×2); cover them, fold back the top flap, and glue the 2 cards facing each other [3].

Calculate the cards for the short sides: 12.9 × 5.6 cm (×2), cover them, fold back the top and the short sides' overlaps, and glue them inside the box. Calculate the bottom card (length – 2 mm × width – 2 mm): 18.9 × 13 cm; cover it, fold back all the overlaps, and glue it to the bottom of the box [4].

Calculate the lid
Measure the length and width of the covered box [4]. The lid is a box whose base is equal to L + 0.7 cm × W + 0.3 cm, so for our box: (19.8 + 0.7 cm)= 20.5 cm × (13.7 + 0.3 cm) = 14 cm.

For the height, a fitted lid is never very high, 3 or 4 cm maximum for big boxes. Here the box is small, so 2 cm will be enough.

Cut out the lid according to the measurements given at the beginning of the chapter and construct it (referring to the 6 steps for making a rectangular box).

Covering the lid
You can cover the lid in the same way as the box, but there is a way of covering the outside, the sides, and the inside at the same time.

1   2   3   4

So cut out a piece of cloth that covers the top + twice the height of the lid on each side (do not forget that there are 2 sides!), + 3 cm of overlap on the bottom of the lid.

For our lid, which measures 20.5 × 14.4 cm × 2 cm, I need to cut out a piece of fabric 20.5 × 2 × (2 + 2) + 3 = 31.5 cm × 14.4 + 2 x (2 + 2) + 3 = 25.4 cm.

Glue the fabric properly centered onto the lid and glue the two large sides. Cut the fabric according to Diagram 1 and glue the two small tongues onto the short sides (5 & 6).

Fold the large overlaps inside the lid and cut them according to photo 9 of the hinged box, then glue them to the insides of the large sides and onto the inside base of the lid.

Glue the exterior of the two small sides and cut away the surplus fabric (7). Recut the overlaps and glue them onto the interior short sides.

All that's left to do is to make a piece for the interior of the lid (interior length of the lid – 2 mm × width – 2 mm): 19.8 × 13.8 cm; cover the card, fold back the 4 overlaps, and glue it in place (8).

A little box that is ideal for storing old lace

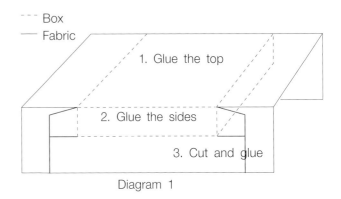

- - - Box
— Fabric

1. Glue the top

2. Glue the sides

3. Cut and glue

Diagram 1

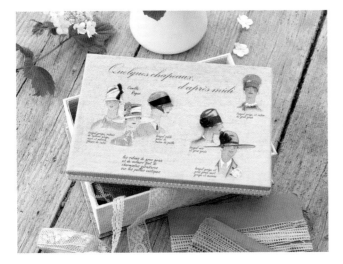

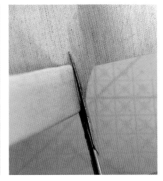

5

6

7

8

[Advice]

The first piece of advice that I give to a beginner is to be sure that you make your boxes in the same way as I do so that you won't get lost in all the measurements.

At the beginning of each box I give all the measurements for cutting out the cardboard. It's best to do your cutting out as you go along to make sure, at each step, that the measurements I've given you match your box. And don't forget to square off your cardboard each time you cut it.

You will have noticed that I never give the dimensions for the card pieces intended for the insides. Go to the chapter on techniques to see how these pieces are calculated. I do provide measurements in metric because that gives the best results for these projects.

When you use fine or light-colored fabric, it might be necessary to stick white cards on the exteriors of the box before covering it.

For the overlaps around the cards, I usually plan for 1.5 cm. I'll let you know if you need more.

When we glue skivertex onto skivertex, you will need to slightly sand down the two surfaces for the glue to adhere properly.

When we have assemblies where the sides are not perpendicular with one another (the assembly of an

octagonal box, for example), it is necessary to sand the edges of the sides so that they align properly [1].

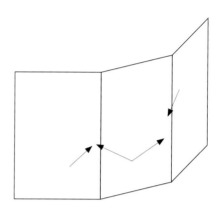

When we work on rounded boxes, you will have to pink the covering. With cards you can pink up to the limit of the card; however, with cardboard, you have to think about the thickness of the edge and therefore pink at 2 mm from the edge of the cardboard [2].

When we cover a rounded box (see the round tea box), apply glue to the card and roll it onto the fabric or skivertex in a manner so that it is properly taut and that the card takes on its final shape [3].

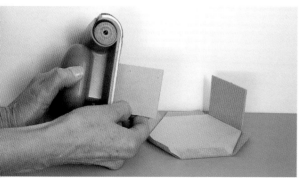

1

2

3

[Monogrammed box]

Who doesn't have old sheets embroidered with lovely monograms hiding away in the attic? This is a simple box to enhance some embroidery my grandmother did.

MATERIALS
› Some pretty embroidery or monogram in a corner if possible
› Gray cardboard 2 mm thick
› Cardstock
› Felting
› Imitation animal fur paper
› Small flat magnets (optional)

CUTTING OUT THE CARDBOARD
› Bottom: 20.8 × 20.8 cm (cut out following Diagram 1)
› Large back: 21.2 × 6.5 cm
› Large sides: 15.5 × 6.5 cm (×2)
› Small sides: 7.5 × 6.5 cm (×2)
› Small front: 10.5 × 6.5 cm
› Lid: 28 × 22 cm (cut out following Diagram 2)

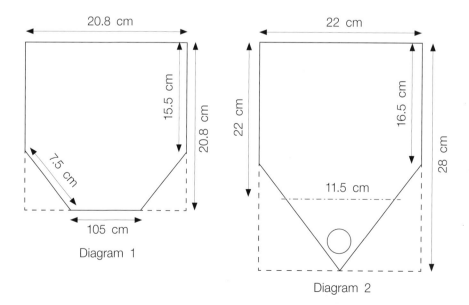

Diagram 1

Diagram 2

PROJECT

MAKING THE BOX

If you wish to add a magnet, slightly hollow out the front of the cardboard and glue the magnet in place before making the box. Do the same with the lid. It isn't necessary to add magnets since the box closes properly without them.

Lightly sand the spines of the sides (see advice on page 10) and make the box with all the sides juxtaposed (1).

COVERING THE BOX

Exceptionally, the box has only an interior hinge; therefore you can cover all around the box in one go. Cut a 82 × 10 cm band out of the imitation-fur paper. The decorations were done with a Big Shot.

If you are doing the same decorations, glue a piece of white fabric where you will be cutting them out, and then glue the band all around the box. Fold the top flap back into the box and the bottom flap back onto the base. Make a piece for the outside base.

Do the interior hinge. Cut a 21 × 12 cm band out of the paper and glue it inside the back of the box. You should also glue it along the edge (2).

Cover the insides with thin cards (see page 5 of the Techniques chapter).

LID

Cut out the lid and incise along the red line with a box cutter. Glue a band of Kraft paper along the fold.

Cut out a piece of felting the size of the top of the lid.

Cut out a piece of the imitation-fur paper the size of the lid, plus 2 cm of overlap on each side if your embroidery has openwork (3).

Assemble the pieces, glue the paper onto the front part, and fold back all the overlaps. Glue the embroidery onto the paper and fold down the edges.

If your monogram doesn't have openwork, you can glue it directly to the lid without the paper underneath.

Glue the interior hinge to the underside of the lid; the lid should overlap the box on all sides, including the back (4).

Make a piece for the front of the inside of the lid and a piece for the bottom of the lid (I found a transfer in an exhibition, and I appliquéd it by iron onto my fabric).

1

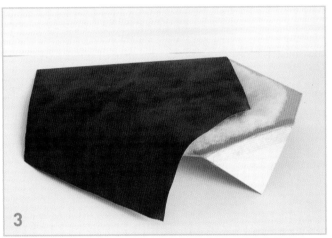

2

3

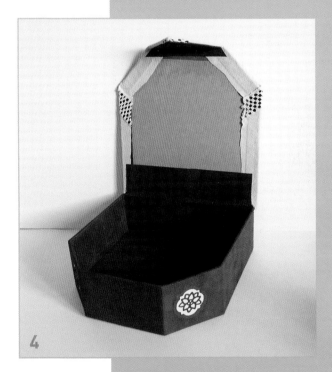

4

[1920s box with a sliding lid]

At flea markets we find all sorts of antique engravings reproduced on paper or, as in this case, fabric.

MATERIALS
> A 1920s image on fabric 21 × 28 cm
> Gray cardboard 2 mm thick
> Cardstock
> Khaki and bronze paper
> Filigree stamping

CUTTING OUT THE CARDBOARD
> Bottom: 24.5 × 18.6 cm
> Large sides: 24.5 × 6 cm (×2)
> Small back: 18.6 × 5.8 cm
> Small front: 18.36 × 5.8 cm

Rims
> Rims for the large sides: 24.5 × 0.5 cm (×2)
> Back rim: 18.1 × 0.5 cm

Interior sides (to be adjusted)
> Uprights sides: 24.2 × 5 cm (×2)
> Uprights back and front: 18.2 × 5 cm (×2)

Lid (to be adjusted)
> 25.2 × 18.5 cm (×2)

PROJECT

MAKING THE BOX

Make the box (see page 5: rectangular box). Glue bands of Kraft paper to the rims of the two large sides and the back to reinforce them (1).

COVERING THE EXTERIOR

Plan for a band of paper that goes all around the box plus 2 cm (90 × 10 cm) or, like I did, several bands in 2 different-colored paper: 20 × 10 cm (×2) of the light paper, and 15 × 10 cm (×2) of the darker paper. Note: we cover the rims at the same time: Diagram 1.

For this leave only 1 cm under the box so as to have the remaining 3 cm at the top to cover the rims.

The corners are a bit difficult to cover! For the back, cut the paper following Diagram 2, for the front copy the photo (2).

Finish the exterior by the base with a card piece.

COVERING THE INTERIOR

Cover the bottom of the box with cardstock. The sides are done in 2 mm cardboard and serve as supports for the lid. Adjust them and cover them, leaving an overlap of 1 cm at the top. Glue the overlaps and then glue these supports on the inside of the box (3).

LID

Adjust the two pieces of cardboard of the lid; they should slide easily.

Cut out the front following Diagram 3.

Cover them with an overlap of 1.5 cm on all sides. Glue the overlaps and glue the two pieces back to back (4).

You can also add a pompom between the two pieces before gluing them together.

Glue on the decorations.

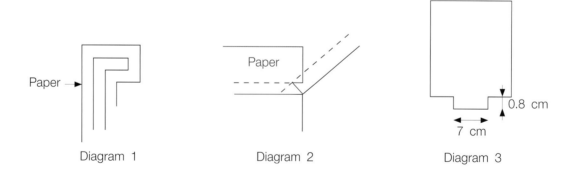

Diagram 1   Diagram 2   Diagram 3

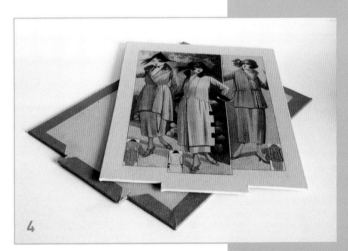

[Watch box]

A box for presenting a lovely watch, but it can be interpreted in a thousand different ways.

MATERIALS
› An engraving of a watch
› Gray cardboard 2 mm thick
› Card 0.7 mm thick
› Cardstock
› Skivertex
› A fastener
› Filigree stamping

CUTTING OUT THE CARDBOARD
› Bottom of the box and lid: 14.4 × 10.2 cm (×2)
› Large sides cut out following Diagram 1: 14.4 × 6 cm (× 4)
› Small back of the box and front of the lid: 10.2 × 5.8 cm (× 2)
› Small front of the box and back of the lid: 10.2 × 2.3 cm (× 2)
› Interior sides of the box: 13.8 × 6.2/2.8 cm (× 2)
› Interior back of the box: 6.2 × 9.4 cm
› Interior front of the box: 2.8 × 9.4 cm

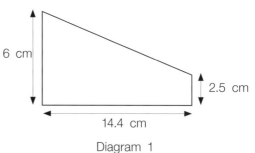

Diagram 1

PROJECT

MAKING AND COVERING THE BOX AND LID

Make the box and lid (see page 5).

The box has a small side in front (10.2 × 2.3 cm) and the lid has a large side in front (10.2 × 5.8 cm) (1).

COVERING THE BOX AND THE LID

Cut out 2 bands, 44 × 9 cm and glue them around the circumference (the two large sides and the front), fold the 2 cm overlaps onto the back, and fold the others into the box and onto the base (2).

THE HINGES

Make the interior hinge for the box: cut out a band of skivertex 10.2 × 12 cm; glue it on the back of the interior of the box and along the edge.

Make the exterior hinge for the lid: cut out a band of skivertex 105 × 12 cm; glue it on the back of the exterior of the lid. Add the two parts of the fasteners (3).

Cut a card (the 0.7 mm card) 10.6 × 14.4 cm and remove the center to make a frame (in this example, I opened the center at 1.3 cm from the edge). Cover the card with skivertex and fold in the center overlaps on each side. Glue the engraving to the top of the lid and then glue the frame over it (4).

COVERING THE INSIDE OF THE BOX AND LID

Cover the two sides and the front with cardstock—the back will be covered by the interior hinge. Prepare the bases but don't glue them.

Cover the bottom of the box with a card piece and the sides with cardboard that overlaps 0.5 cm. Cover the cardboard, leaving an overlap of 2 cm at the top and 1.5 cm on the side (5). Pay attention at the corners!

ASSEMBLING THE BOX AND THE LID

Glue the exterior lid hinge to the back of the box and fold the flap under the base. Leave it to dry properly. Then glue the interior box hinge to the inside back of the lid (6 & 7).

All that's left to do is to glue the prepared card to the interior of the lid and make a card for the exterior base of the box.

This box was made for a steampunk pocket watch. If you have a classical watch, make a cushion with 0.7 mm card and stuffing. Cover it with fabric or velvet.

You can also make a window to show off the watch instead of an engraving. In this case you should glue on a glass window.

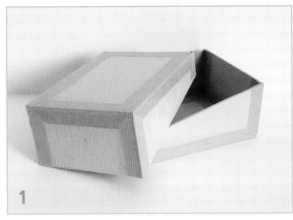

1

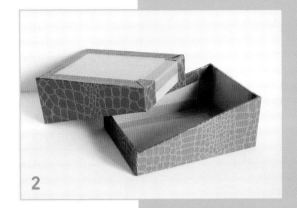

3

2

4

5

6

7

[Display box]

This can be used to keep your keys in, or for the necklaces of good little girls.

MATERIALS
> An old engraving (optional) 13.6 × 9.6 cm
> Gray cardboard 2 mm
> Cardstock
> White damask skivertex
> Pink paper
> 1 doorknob
> Small decorative accessories (optional)

CUTTING OUT THE CARDBOARD
Little box
> Bottom: 14.6 × 10.2 cm
> Large sides: 14.6 × 1.4 cm (× 2)
> Small sides: 10.2 × 1.2 cm (× 2)

Box and lid
> Bottom and lid: 22 × 17.6 cm (× 2)
> Large sides (box): 25 × 5 cm (× 2)
> Small sides (box): 17.6 × 4.8 cm (× 2)
> Large sides (lid): 22 × 1.5 cm (× 2)
> Small sides (lid): 17.6 × 1.3 cm (× 2)

> Interior uprights of the box (to be checked): 21.5 × 5.8 cm (× 2) and 17.2 × 5.8 cm (× 2)

> Interior base of the lid (to be checked): 21.5 × 17.5 cm

PROJECT

ASSEMBLY

Cut out a frame in the box, 13.6 × 9.6 cm (Diagram 1).

Make the box, the lid, and the little box (see page 5: rectangular box) [1].

COVERING THE BOX

Cover three sides of the exterior of the box (1 long side and the two short sides) and fold the 2 cm overlaps onto the second long side, as shown in Diagram 2.

Make the interior hinge with a band of skivertex 21.5 × 10 cm and glue it to the long side that hasn't been covered leaving an overlap of 4 cm [2].

Cover the bottom of the box with a card piece.

Check the interior uprights; cover them, leaving an overlap of 2 cm at the top and 1.5 cm on each side—pay attention to the visible corners. Glue them to the four sides of the box (they should fit snugly, allowing room for the lid) [3].

COVERING THE LID

Cut out a piece of skivertex, 30 × 30 cm, and glue it to the lid so that you have an overlap of 4 cm on three sides and 8 cm on the fourth (long) side, which will be the exterior hinge.

Open the center and fold the overlaps toward the inside. Glue the 4 cm overlap to the long side and cut out the angles (see page 5: box with a fitted lid) [4].

The 2 tongues are glued to the short sides of the lid. Fold the long side inside the lid.

Do the same on the other long side, but don't fold the skivertex into the lid (it's the hinge) [5].

Glue the two short sides, recut the surplus close to the edge, and fold the overlaps inside.

ASSEMBLING THE BOX AND THE LID

Place the lid onto the box, making sure that the inside hinge is folded inside the box. First of all, glue the exterior hinge, leaving it to dry properly before gluing the interior hinge (see page 5: assembling a hinge) [6].

Cover the base of the box with a card piece.

COVERING THE LITTLE BOX

Glue the little box to a rectangle of pink paper 21 × 6 cm.

Glue the sides in the same way as you did for the lid (first the 2 long sides with the angles cut and then the 2 short sides), but don't fold the overlaps inside the little box.

Use cardstock for the bottom of the little box. On the sides, place cardboard between 2 to 3 mm from the top, if you are using glass for the window, or 1 mm from the top if you are using Plexiglas. Install your decorations and place the glass or Plexiglas [7].

Check that the base card (21.5 × 17.5 cm) for the bottom of the interior of the lid fits snugly, and adjust if necessary. Measure the little box (exterior measurements) and cut the measurements out of the base card (14.7 × 10.7 cm to be double checked). Cover one side of the base card, fold the four sides inside, and cut the surplus close to the edges.

Pass the little box through the hole and glue the overlaps of the little box to the base card. Put the glass in place and glue it all to the interior of the lid [8].

You can embellish the top of your box with a little frame, as I have, made of cardboard (23.5 × 19 cm); open the center at 1.5 cm from the edge, covered and glued to the box.

Add the tiny doorknob and your box is ready to be hung on the wall as a box for your keys or a jewelry box for little girls. In this case, cut out 3 pieces of cardboard (17 × 2.5 cm), glue them one on top of the other, cover them and glue them to the upper short side of the interior of the box, and add 3 little hooks [9].

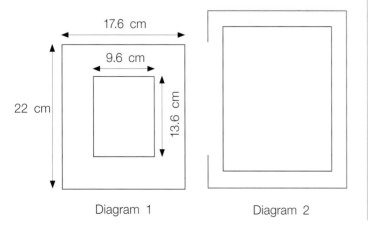

17.6 cm

9.6 cm

22 cm

13.6 cm

Diagram 1   Diagram 2

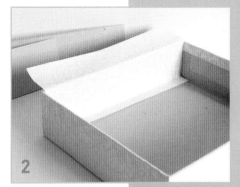

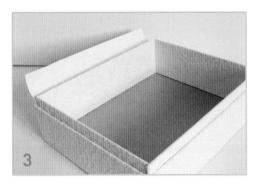

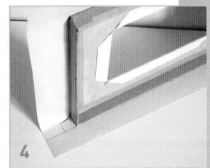

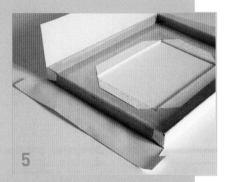

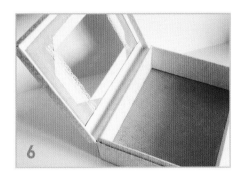

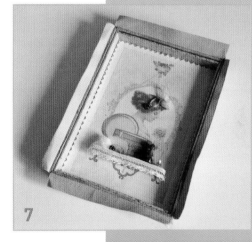

[Candy box]

For the exterior, you should use paper instead of fabric because fabric will fray.

MATERIALS
› Gray cardboard 2 mm
› Card 0.7 mm
› Cardstock
› Light-green velvet paper
› Japanese paper
› Porcelain doorknob (from dressmakers' flea markets)

CUTTING OUT THE CARDBOARD
› 1 circle, radius 5 cm, for the bottom of the box
› Lids (see details further on)

The 0.7 mm card:
› For the upright: 32 × 10 cm (to be adjusted)
› For the outer cover: 33 × 10 cm (to be adjusted)

PROJECT

MAKING THE BOX

First, pink a band of Kraft paper and glue it so it overlies the bottom of the box.

Glue the 0.7 mm card (for the upright) and place around the base. The short sides of the band should be edge to edge; adjust if necessary and glue a band of Kraft to keep them together. Glue bands of Kraft inside the box [1].

COVERING THE EXTERIOR

Adjust the 0.7 mm outer card; the short sides should be edge to edge. Cover it with the velvet paper, leaving an overlap of 1.5 cm all round; fold a short side inward.

Glue this band to the outside of the box, first gluing the short side that doesn't have the fold (be sure that the joins on the box are opposite the joins on the outer cover). Fold the top of the cover inside the box at the top and under the base at the bottom [2].

Cut a 35 × 16 cm band out of the Japanese paper.

Cut cards 35 × 13 cm and glue it to the back of the Japanese paper between the red lines in Diagram 1 (it will be easier to spread the glue on the back of the Japanese paper and place the card onto the paper). Cut out the vertical lines with a box cutter (they are 1.5 cm apart) and mark the folds.

Glue the bottom band on the very edge of the base of the box, adjust the length, and glue the pinked part underneath the box. Leave it to dry properly [3].

Glue the top band on the very edge of the top of the box and fold the pinked part inside the box [4].

Make the exterior base out of cardstock.

COVERING THE INTERIOR

Make the bottom out of cardstock. Prepare a piece for the interior of the box (31 × 9.8 cm; to be adjusted), spread glue on the card and roll it to tighten the fabric, fold back the 2 long sides and one short side, and glue it inside the box.

LID

This is made up or a series on circles in 2 mm cardboard, alternatively covered in Japanese paper and velvet paper.

From the bottom to the top:

2 circles with a radius of 4.2 cm (check this—it must enter into the box)

3 circles with a radius of 5.2 cm (check this—it should sit on the box)

Perhaps another 3 smaller circles for decoration. Screw the porcelain doorknob in place (or another type of decorative knob) [5].

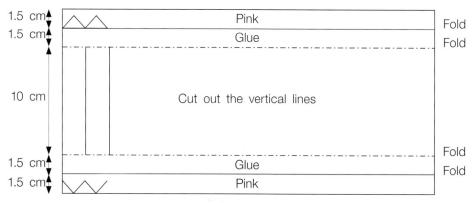

Diagram 1

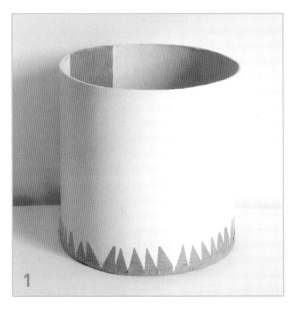

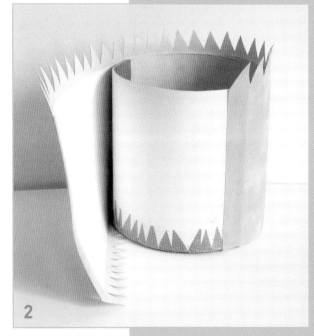

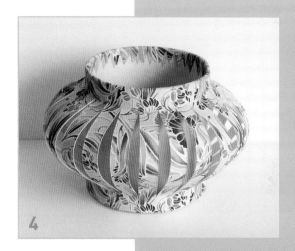

[Sheathed knitting needle case]

MATERIALS
› Gray cardboard 2 mm
› Cardstock
› Skivertex
› Fabric

CUTTING OUT THE CARDBOARD
Box
› Bottom: 43 × 8.5 cm
› Large sides: 43 × 5.2 cm (× 2)
› Small sides: 8.5 × 5 cm (× 2)

Sheath
› Bottom: 43 × 9.3 cm
› Large sides: 43 × 5.8 cm (× 2)
› Top: 43 × 9.7 cm

PROJECT

MAKING AND COVERING THE BOX

Make the box (see techniques on page 5).

Cover the 4 exterior sides. If you are covering it with skivertex, you should cover it in two parts: cut out a 56 × 8 cm band of skivertex, glue it to 2 sides and turn the overlaps in, then cut out another 56 × 8 cm band and glue it to the other two sides, which should touch the edge of the first band without covering it. Turn the overlaps into the box and under the base (1).

Cover with cardstock for the interior (2).

MAKING AND COVERING THE SHEATH

Place the two sides on the bottom and keep them in place with bands of Kraft.

To make things easier, you will cover the interior of the sheath before doing the exterior. Cut a 43 × 22 cm band out of the skivertex and glue it to the three interior sides without touching the two ends, so that you can fold in the outside overlaps. Be careful to mark the spines with a folding knife.

Cut a 43 × 9.7 cm band out of the skivertex and glue it to the top side without touching the two ends (3).

Stick the top side with the cover on the inside to the other three sides with bands of kraft.

Cut a 45 × 34 cm band out of the skivertex and glue it all round the sheath. Cut the surplus so that the edge touches, without covering the first edge. Fold the overlaps on the short sides inward over the interior cover and glue them down (4).

Cut a 43 × 4 cm band out of the rigidex or 0.7 mm card (easier) (adjust the measurements according to your decoration). Cover it with a band of felting (optional) between the card and the fabric. Fold the long sides under the card and glue it to the top of the sheath. Fold the short sides inside. I glue a small piece of skivertex to the short sides to stop the fabric from fraying (4).

I also made two small bands that I glued to each side of the sheath.

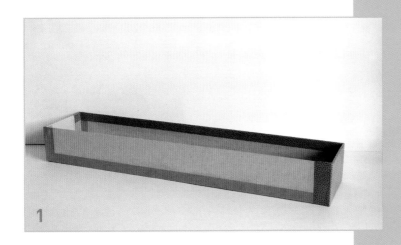

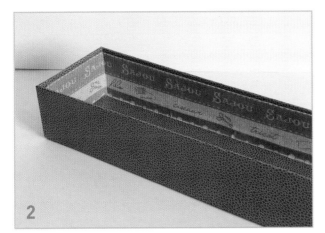

[Biscuit box]

This box is a copy of a biscuit box that was highly fashionable in the 1930s. They were very often made of glass or crystal with a wooden top. It's a very simple box: it's the little details, as always, that add to its charm.

MATERIALS
› Gray cardboard 2 mm
› Card 0.7 mm
› Cardstock
› Fabric
› Papers
› Handles
› 2 decorative brads

CUTTING OUT THE CARBOARD
› Bottom of the box: 23.6 × 16.6 cm to be recut according to Diagram 1
› Long sides: 10.6 × 6 cm (× 4)
› Short sides: 5.6 × 6 cm (× 4)
› Lid to be recut: 24 × 17 cm (Diagram 1 with 6 cm on the small sides)
› Top of the lid to be recut: 22 × 15 cm (Diagram 1 with 5 cm)
› Underside of the lid to be recut: 23 × 16 cm (Diagram 1 with 5.5 cm)
› Tray to be recut: 26 × 19 cm (Diagram 1 with 7 cm)
› Decorations: 6.5 × 5.7 cm (× 8)
› Decorations: 6.5 × 1 cm (× 8)

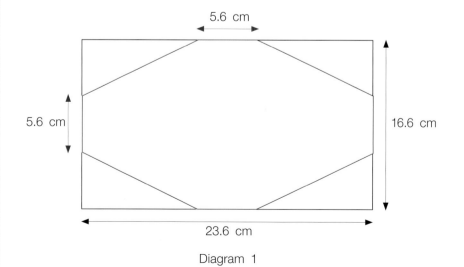

Diagram 1

PROJECT

MAKING AND COVERING THE BOX

Make the box, with all the sides juxtaposed after sanding them down (see "advice" page 10).

Cut a 70 × 9 cm band out of the fabric and glue it all around the box. Fold the overlaps inside the box and under the base. If you want to center your patterns like I did, cover only the long sides. In this case, don't forget to cover the top edges of the short sides [1].

Add cardstock for the interior [2].

DECORATING THE BOX

Glue the 6.5 × 5.7 cm cardboard pieces 2 by 2. Cover them and fold under the overlaps (when you have several thicknesses of cardboard to cut the corners of the cover in right angles) [3].

Cover the 8 6.5 × 1 cm cardboards, tuck under the overlaps, and glue them on the previously made decorations, with a space between them of about 2 cm.

Screw handles onto two of them, and on the other two add a filigree stamping or another decoration.

Glue the 4 decorations to the four short sides of the box [4 & 5].

THE LID

Check the lid—it should sit perfectly on the top of the box and between the decorations. Cover it with paper and carefully fold the overlaps underneath.

Cover the top of the lid in fabric, fold the overlaps underneath, and glue it to the top of the lid. Put it under a weight.

Make the handle with 3 × 0.7 mm cards:
– 1.6 × 10.5 cm folded at 1.6 cm from the edge and covered in brown paper.
– 1 × 10.5 cm folded at 1.6 cm from the edge and covered in blue paper.
– 1 × 7.3 cm for underneath the handle, covered in blue paper.

Glue the three pieces together and glue the extremities to the box, add the 2 decorative brads, and fix them on the underside with Kraft [6].

Check that the underneath of the lid fits into the box properly, cover it, fold the overlaps under it, and then glue it to the underside of the lid.

THE TRAY

Cover the top side of the tray with paper or skivertex and use cardstock for the underside.

Glue the box to the tray and put it under a weight until dry.

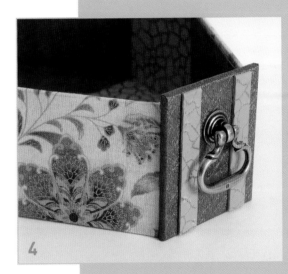

[Cake stand]

A cake stand for your cupcakes. I covered it in coated cotton fabric, which makes it easier to clean. A word of advice: don't use plastic tablecloth material, which is thicker and doesn't give satisfactory results.

MATERIALS
› Gray cardboard 2 mm
› Backing board 3 mm
› Cardstock
› Coated cotton fabric
› Skivertex
› Paint

CUTTING OUT THE 2 MM CARDBOARD
Cut out each tray twice
› The large tray: see Fig. 1
› Draw a circle with a 14 cm radius. On the diameter in the same center, draw a circle with a 7 cm radius and 2 of the same size at points A and B.
› At points C, D, E, F, which are at the intersections of the precedent circles, draw 4 circles of 7 cm radius.
› Cut out your pattern, following the red lines.
› The second tray: do the same, with the circle at 10 cm radius and the inner ones at 5 cm radius.
› The small tray: repeat the operation with a radius of 6 cm and the inner circles at 3 cm (1)

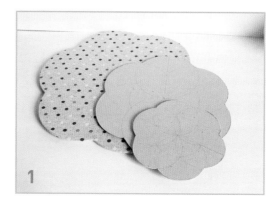

CUTTING OUT THE 3 MM CARDBOARD
The legs are cut out of the white 3 mm backing board: see Fig. 2
› The bottom legs: 16/6 x 10 cm (x 2)
› Middle legs: 10/4.5 x 10 cm (x 2)
› Top legs: 6/2.5 x 8 cm (x 2)
› Cut out the center part on the top of one leg and the bottom of the other so that they fit together perfectly (Figs. 2 & 3)

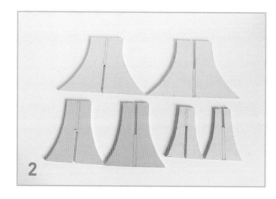

PROJECT

COVERING THE TRAYS

Cover the top cardboard of the trays with the coated cotton fabric [4]. For pinking, see advice on page 10.

On the underneath tray, cut out a cross the dimension of the feet that will be set in it (6 cm for the bottom tray, 4.5 cm for the middle tray, and 2.5 cm for the top tray). Cover them in skivertex [4].

Glue the two parts of each tray together underside against underside and put them under a weight until dry.

COVERING THE LEGS

Paint the spines of each leg.

Glue skivertex to one side, cutting it flush with the edges of the legs and with the edges of the slit.

Glue skivertex to the other side and cut it flush with the edges [5].

Glue the legs to each tray. I decided not to glue the three elements together so that I can present them aligned or slightly off-center. However, for better stability, you can glue the three levels one on top of the other.

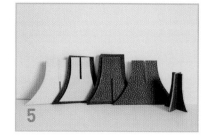

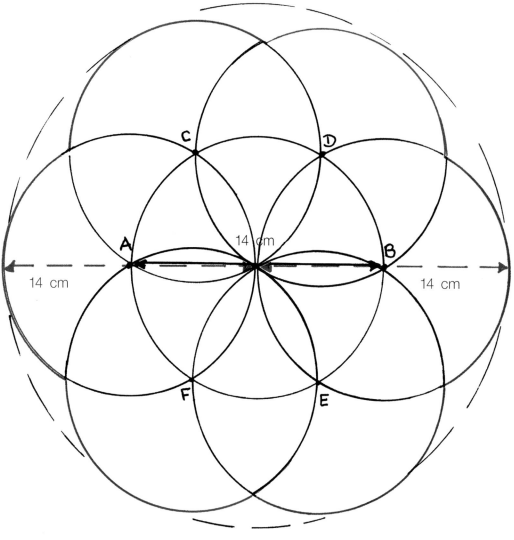

Template 1

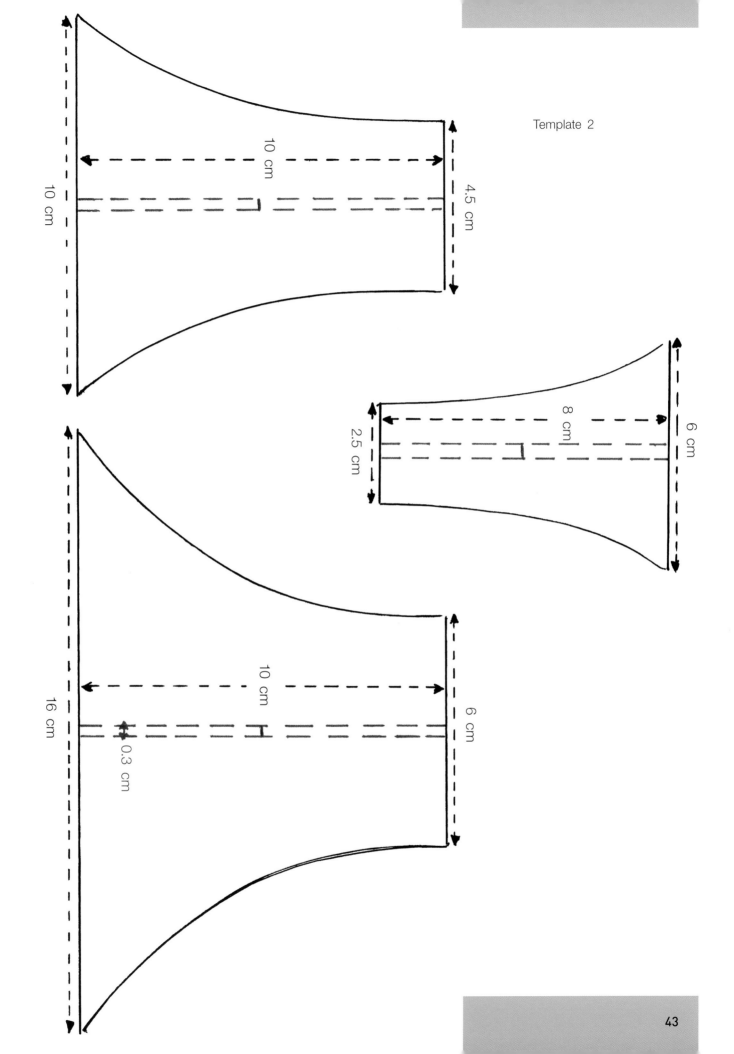

Template 2

[Square tea box]

MATERIALS
› Gray cardboard 2 mm
› Cardstock
› Skivertex and paper
› A pompom and 4 buttons

CUTTING OUT THE CARDBOARD
Box
› Bottom: 10 x 9.6 cm
› Large sides: 10 x 10 cm (x 2)
› Small sides: 9.6 x 9.8 cm (x 2)
› Decorations: 8 x 8 cm (x 4)
› Decorations: 7 x 7 cm (x 4)
› Interior: 9.5 x 9.2 cm (x 2)
› Interior: 9.1 x 9.2 cm (x 2)

Lid
› Base of the lid: 9.6 x 9.6 cm
› 4 pieces of cardboard cut out
  according to Diagram 1
› Bottom interior: 9.4 x 9.4 cm

Large plinth
› Base of the plinth: 10.6 x 10.6 cm
› 4 pieces of cardboard cut out
  according to Diagram 2
› Bottom exterior: 11.5 x 11.5 cm

Small plinth
› Base of the plinth: 8.1 x 8.1 cm
› 4 pieces of cardboard cut out
  according to Diagram 3
› Bottom exterior: 9 x 9 cm
› Between the 2 plinths: 4 x 4 cm

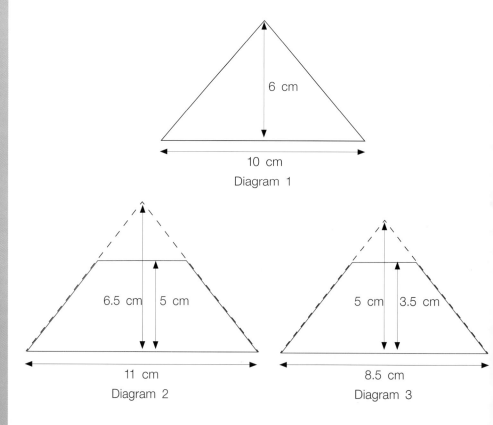

6 cm

10 cm
Diagram 1

6.5 cm 5 cm

11 cm
Diagram 2

5 cm 3.5 cm

8.5 cm
Diagram 3

PROJECT

MAKING AND COVERING THE BOX

Make the box (see techniques on page 5).

Cut a 43 × 13 cm band out of the skivertex and glue it around the box. Tuck the top overlaps inside the box and the bottom ones under the base (1). Cover the 8 × 8 cm decorations with black skivertex and the 7 × 7 cm decorations with fancy paper.

Glue them to the center of each side of the box (2).

Interior of the box: I chose to make the insides out of cardboard rather than out of cardstock, so that the box seals more closely to conserve all of the tea's aroma. The cardboard under the lid will rest on these pieces of cardboard.

Check the 4 pieces of cardboard for the interior and adjust them if necessary.

Cover the bottom with cardstock; the overlaps fold back against the sides of the box. Cover the 4 pieces of cardboard flush on 3 sides and with an overlap of 1.5 cm at the top; fold these overlaps onto the back of the cardboard and glue them down (2).

MAKING AND COVERING THE LID AND THE PLINTHS

The lid and the two plinths are made in the same way.

Cut out the center of each base 2 cm from the edge and add strengthening bands of Kraft.

Flatten all the spines of the base and the 4 sides of each element with the scraper (see advice on page 10).

Mount all the sides next to the base cardboard. Glue bands of Kraft along the spines both inside and out.

Prepare cardstock pieces to cover the 4 triangles (or trapezium). Cover them with skivertex, with 1.5 cm overlaps. Place 2 cards facing each other, with the overlaps folded underneath and the 2 others with the overlaps folding obliquely along the spine of the card next to it, before gluing the card in place. Fold the overlaps of each element inside (3).

For the lid, make pieces (7 × 4 cm) and cover them with the decorative paper (3).

Place the pompom at the top of the lid by making a small hole, and glue the ends under the cardboard with Kraft to reinforce it.

Check that the cardboard for the bottom of the lid's interior enters perfectly into the box; cover it in skivertex and glue it under the lid.

For the plinths: cover the 2 exterior bases in skivertex and the small intermediary cardboard with decorative paper. Glue the small plinth to the base and weigh it down; glue the intermediary card to the top of the small plinth.

Glue the base under the large plinth and weigh it down; glue the top of the large plinth to the intermediary card. Check with a level to make sure that everything is in line; otherwise you'll either have to sand down the top of the plinths or compensate with small pieces of card (4).

Glue the box to the plinth; you can add decorative buttons to the box and ribbon between the plinths and their bases.

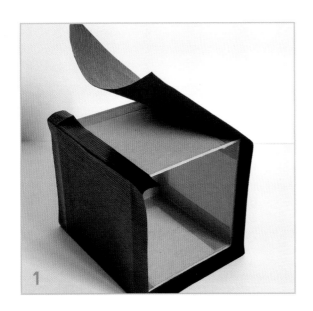

[Art Nouveau tea box]

MATERIALS
› Gray cardboard 2 mm
› Card 0.7 mm
› Cardstock
› Skivertex and decorative paper
› 1 pompom

CUTTING OUT THE CARDBOARD
› 2 circles with a 7.5 cm radius cut out along the red line (Diagram 1) of the box and the lid
› 2 circles with a 7.5 cm radius cut out along the red line (Diagram 2) for the interior cover of the box and the lid
› 2 cardboards according to the model for the plinth
› Top interior: 14.5 x 6.5 cm

CUTTING OUT THE CARD
› For making the box: 29 x 7 cm
› For covering the exterior of the box: 30 x 7 cm
› For covering the interior of the box: 27 x 6.5 cm
› For making the lid: 19 x 7 cm
› For covering the exterior of the lid: 20 x 7 cm
› For covering the interior of the lid: 20 x 6.5 cm
› For making the plinth: 16 x 4.5 cm
› Everything will be adjusted

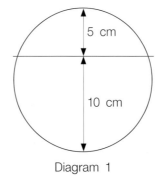

5 cm

10 cm

Diagram 1

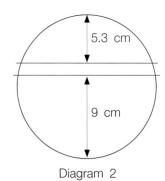

5.3 cm

9 cm

Diagram 2

PROJECT

MAKING THE BOX

Glue two overlapping bands of Kraft on each side of the 0.7 mm card. Pink the edges of the Kraft and glue the 2 sides in 2 mm cardboard to the card (1).

EXTERIOR COVER OF THE BOX

Cut out 2 pieces of cardstock, using the diagram as a guide, but with a diameter of 15.2 cm to cover the two rounded faces of the box. Cover them with the decorative paper, with overlaps of 1.5 cm. Glue the cards to each face, fold the overlaps onto the sides of the card, and fold the top overlap inside the box.

Cut out a skivertex with a diameter of 12.5 cm and a piece of cardstock with a diameter of 12 cm to make the decoration.

Cover the card with paper, fold under the overlaps, and glue the skivertex and the card (2).

Adjust the exterior card and cover it in skivertex with an overlap of 1.5 cm (see advice page 10). Pink the overlaps on the rounded parts and glue them on the inside of the card. Glue the card to the box and fold the two short overlaps inside the box.

COVERING THE INTERIOR OF THE BOX

Adjust and cover the interior card with overlaps of 1.5 cm (it should reach 1 cm from the top; check with the cards cut out according to Diagram 2). Fold the short sides under the card, pink the long sides, and glue the card inside the box.

Cover the half circles with skivertex, flush along the round edge and with an overlap of 1.5 cm at the top. Fold this onto the back and glue the half circles inside the box.

Adjust the top interior, cover it in skivertex and paper, and fold back the overlaps. Place a piece of card under the top cardstock, cover it, tuck in the overlaps, and glue it. Screw in the button (3 & 4).

MAKING AND COVERING THE LID

The lid is made exactly the same way as the box.

Cover the exterior in the same way, being very careful to make sure the decorative circles correspond.

COVERING THE INTERIOR OF THE LID

Adjust the interior card: it should surpass by 3 mm (check with the cards cut out according to Diagram 2). Cover it with skivertex, with overlaps of 1.5 cm. Fold back the short side; be careful, they are seen (3 mm) from the outside, so fold them neatly. Pink the large sides and glue the card inside the lid.

Cover the half circles with skivertex, flush with the rounded parts and with an overlap of 1.5cm at the top. Fold back the top and glue them inside the lid (5).

PLINTH

Make the plinth, with the sides in cardboard cut out following the model side-by-side with the assembly card (mark the edges of the card with a box cutter). Cut out two pieces of cardstock for the front and the back of the plinth and cover them with overlaps of 1.5 cm. Glue them to the plinth and fold back the overlaps.

Make two small 0.7 mm cards 4.5 × 4 cm, adjust the sides, cover them and fold the overlaps onto the card, glue the card in place, and fold the bottom underneath the plinth. There's no need to cover the center; it will be glued under the box (6 & 7).

Make a piece for the bottom exterior of the plinth.

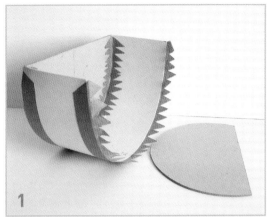

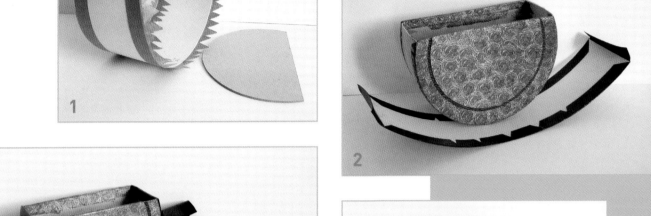

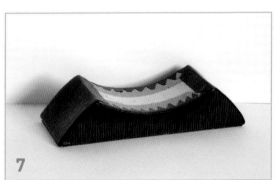

Base Template

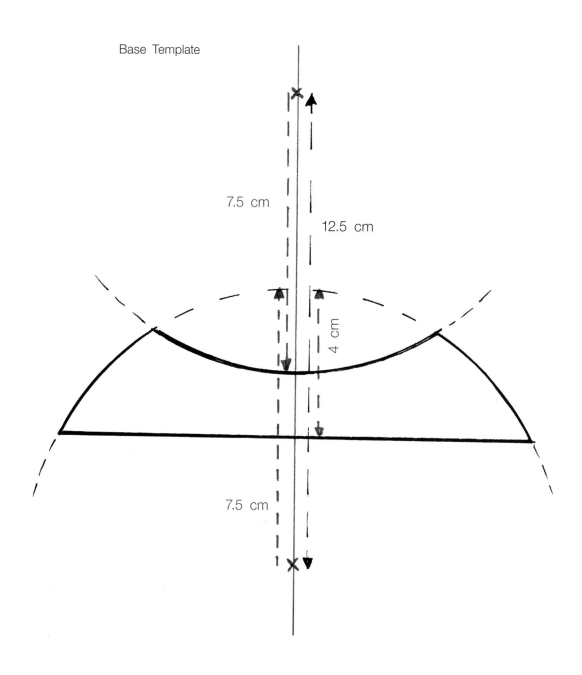

7.5 cm

12.5 cm

4 cm

7.5 cm

[Japanese bowl]

On my last trip to Paris I went to a superb Baccarat exhibition at the Petit Palais, which gave me the idea for this bowl, which can be used as a trinket bowl. Since Japan was very fashionable in the 1920s, I've chosen a brightly colored Japanese fabric.

MATERIALS
› Gray cardboard 2 mm
› Card 0.7 mm
› Cardstock
› Skivertex

CUTTING OUT THE CARDBOARD
› 3 circles 10 cm diameter

CUTTING OUT THE CARD
› 1 circle 30 cm recut according to Template 1
› Number the pieces 1 to 4 and copy them onto a 0.7 mm card

PROJECT

MAKING THE CUP

Cut out the 0.7 mm card, dampen it, and leave it to dry out in a salad bowl so that it takes on a rounded shape (1).

EXTERIOR COVER

Cover each side separately, with overlaps of 1.5 cm, which are folded inside the sides. Glue small pieces of fabric between the cards to hide the visible edges of the bottom of the bowl and reinforce the folds with bands of Kraft (2).

Prepare 8 pieces of skivertex 9 × 8.5 cm and glue them 2 by 2, underside against underside. Cut each out following Template 2. Glue them

between the cards at 2 cm from the top. Take the time to glue one side properly before gluing the other side (3).

Glue the 3 cardboard circles together to make a base. Cover it with a band of fabric and make a circle covered with skivertex for the underside of the base. Glue the base to the bottom of the bowl (3).

INTERIOR COVER

Adjust the second set of 0.7 mm cards so that they are slightly smaller than the first; cover them with 1.5 cm overlaps, which are folded inside. Glue each card in place inside the bowl. Make a circle covered with fabric or skivertex for the bottom of the interior (4).

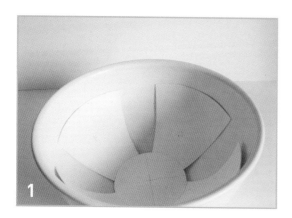

Template 1

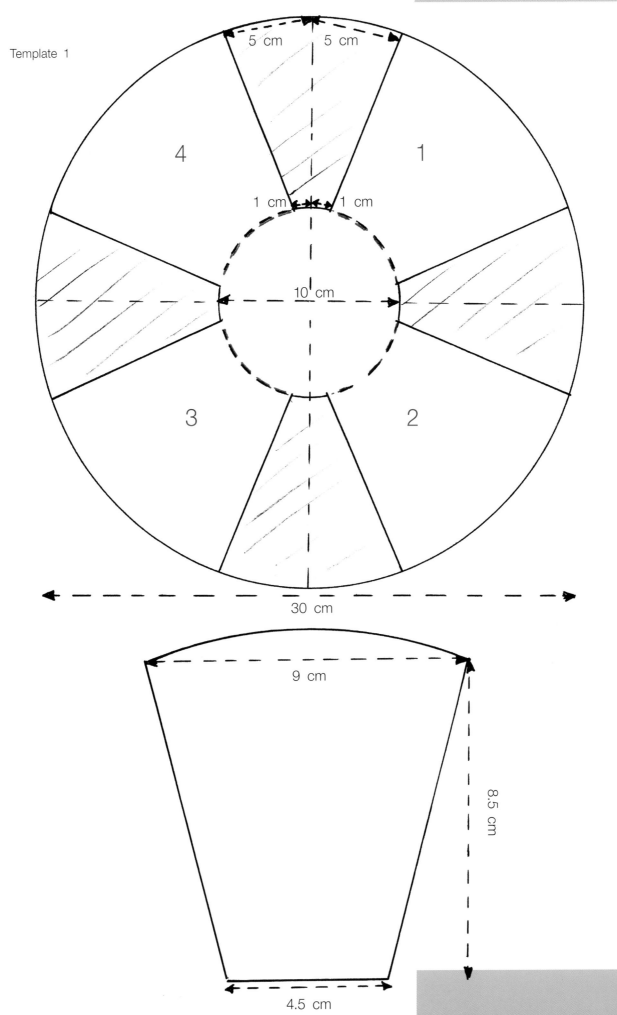

5 cm   5 cm

4   1

1 cm   1 cm

10 cm

3   2

30 cm

9 cm

8.5 cm

4.5 cm

[Boxes for buttons and ribbons]

I felt nostalgic about the series of pots that our grandmothers used for storing flour, coffee, etc. These boxes are adapted for storing, this time, buttons and ribbons or anything else.

MATERIALS
› Gray cardboard 2 mm
› Cardstock
› Linen and paper
› Wooden decorations
› Assortment of buttons and ribbons

LARGE BOX
› Bottom: 7 x 5 cm
› Large sides: 2 x Template 1
› Small sides: 2 x Template 2
› Base: 7 x 5.4 cm

Lid for the Large Box
› Bottom: 12.6 x 10 cm
› Large sides: 2 x Diagram 1
› Small sides: 2 x Diagram 2
› Base: 14 x 12.4 cm

SMALL BOX
› Bottom: 7 x 5 cm
› Large sides: 2 x Template 3
› Small sides: 2 x Template 4
› Base: 7 x 5.4 cm

Lid for the Small Box
› Bottom: 11.6 x 8.8 cm
› Large sides: 2 x Template 3
› Small sides: 2 x Template 4
› Base: 13 x 10.8 cm

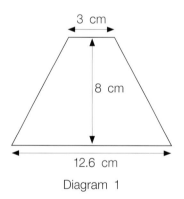

3 cm

8 cm

12.6 cm

Diagram 1

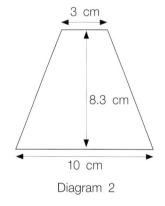

3 cm

8.3 cm

10 cm

Diagram 2

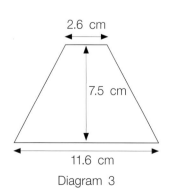

2.6 cm

7.5 cm

11.6 cm

Diagram 3

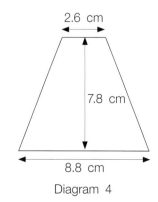

2.6 cm

7.8 cm

8.8 cm

Diagram 4

PROJECT

MAKING THE BOXES

Make a light cut with a box cutter along the lines
-.-.-.- shown in models 1, 2, 3 & 4 to incurve the
top parts of the sides.

Make the boxes with the large sides and the
small sides (see techniques on page 5) [1].

COVERING THE EXTERIOR OF THE BOXES

Cut out paper bands 3 cm wide, fold them in 2 and
glue them to the spines. You will have to do this
in two parts since the paper isn't supple enough
to follow the bend at the top.

Fold the overlaps inside the top and under
the bottom.

In the same way, glue 4 small bands on the
top part of the interior spines; the paper lies flush
at the top and at the bottom [2].

Cut out cardstock following the red lines in
the models. Cover them in linen with overlaps of
1.5 cm, except at the top, where you will need an
overlap of 2 cm. Fold over the overlaps on the large
sides. Glue the cards to each face; fold the overlap
inside the box and the under the bottom.

Cover the base, fold in the overlaps, and glue
it under the box.

COVERING THE INSIDE OF THE BOXES

Cut out the cards for the two large sides following
the models, with 2 mm less on the sides and 1.5
cm at the top. Try them and correct if necessary.
Cover them with overlaps of 1.5 cm, fold in the
top, and glue them to the two large sides (the same
principle as for the rectangular box in the techniques
chapter on page 5). Do the same for the pieces on
the small sides, folding the overlaps on the sides
and the top [3].

Use cardstock for the bottom interior.

LID

Sand the 4 edges of the bottom of the lid and the
bottom of the 4 sides (see advice on page 10).

Make the lid with the large sides and the small
sides. Measure the hole at the top and cut out a
piece of cardstock, glue it in place, and reinforce
it with small bands of Kraft [4].

Cover the 2 small sides with linen and fold
back the overlaps on all sides.

Cut out pieces for the large sides, cover them,
fold the overlaps on the sides, glue them to the
lid, and fold the overlaps into the lid and under
the bottom.

Cut the decorative pieces and cover them with
paper. Fold in the overlaps and glue them [5].

The measurements of the cards are general;
you will have to adapt them for your lids. Make a
piece for the top of the lid.

Check that the base of the lid sits perfectly on
the cards inside the box, and correct where necessary.

Cut out a small piece of card for the top of the
lid. Cover it on one side and fold under the overlaps.
Cover the other side with another piece of cardstock.

Glue it on the top of the lid and add a button on
the top. Mine is a large wooden bead with a mother-
of-pearl bead sitting on it, fixed in place with a pin,
which serves to reinforce the assembly.

Diagrams for the large box:

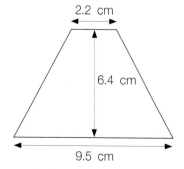

Decorative cards for the large sides

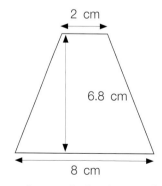

Decorative cards for the small size

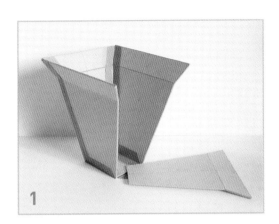

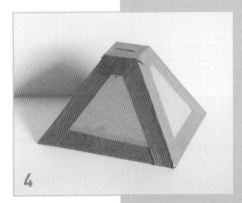

Diagrams for the
small box:

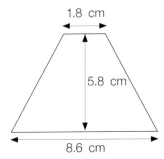

1.8 cm

5.8 cm

8.6 cm

Decorative cards for the
large sides

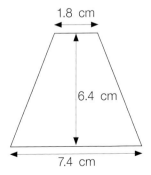

1.8 cm

6.4 cm

7.4 cm

Decorative cards for the
small size sides

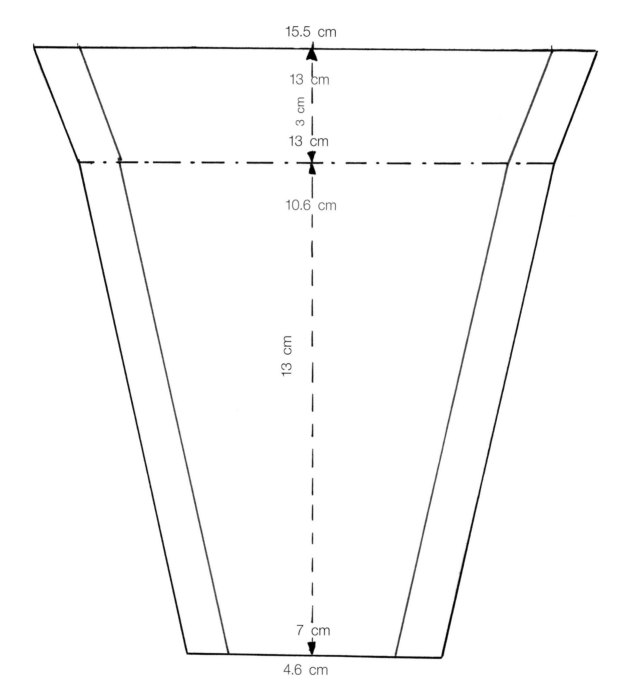

15.5 cm

13 cm

3 cm

13 cm

10.6 cm

13 cm

7 cm

4.6 cm

Template 1

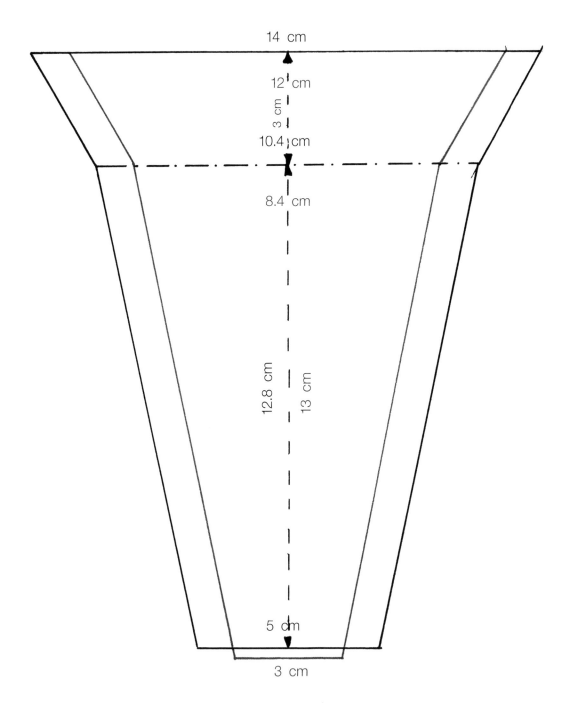

14 cm

12 cm

3 cm

10.4 cm

8.4 cm

12.8 cm

13 cm

5 cm

3 cm

Template 2

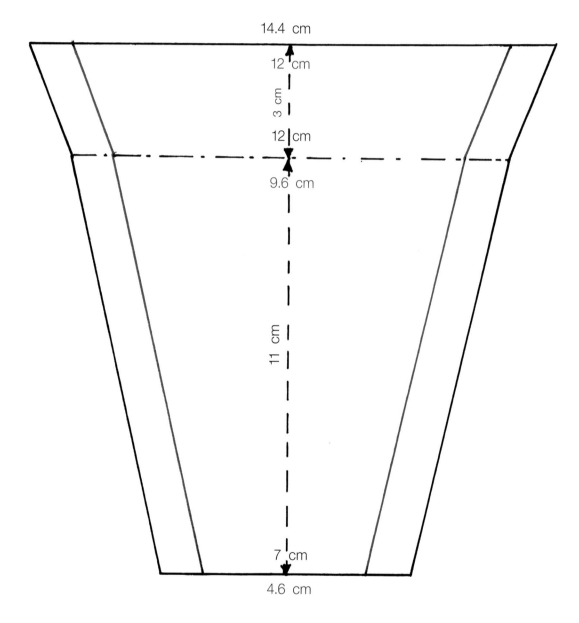

14.4 cm

12 cm

3 cm

12 cm

9.6 cm

11 cm

7 cm

4.6 cm

Template 3

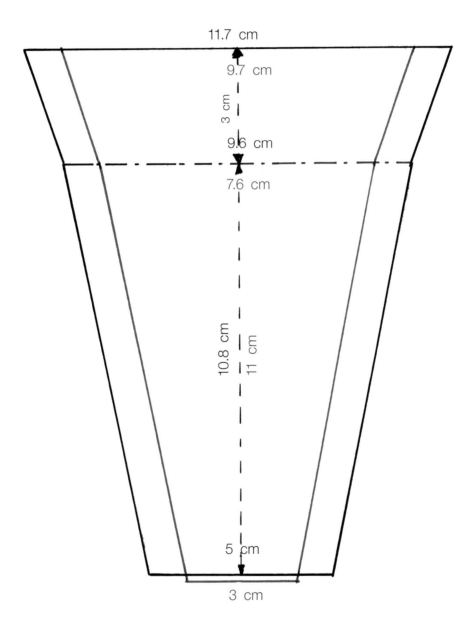

11.7 cm

9.7 cm

3 cm

9.6 cm

7.6 cm

10.8 cm

11 cm

5 cm

3 cm

Template 4

[Psychedelic box]

It's not really the box that's psychedelic; it's the fabric that seems to have leapt out of the 1970s!

MATERIALS
› Gray cardboard 2 mm
› Cardstock
› Card 0.7 mm
› Fabric
› Paper

CUTTING OUT THE CARDBOARD
› Bottom: 14.4 x 14 cm
› Large sides: 14.4 x 7 cm (x 2)
› Small sides: 14 x 6.8 cm (x 2)
› Top: 20 x 20 cm
› Base: 15 x 15 cm
› 3 circles 14.4 cm diameter

CUTTING OUT THE CARD
› 20/14.4 x 8 cm (x 4) to be recut
   following the black lines in the
   model for the assembly
› 19/13.4 x 8 cm (x 4) to be recut
   following the red lines in the model
   for the cover

PROJECT

MAKING AND COVERING THE BOX

Make the box (see techniques on page 5).

You won't cover the outside, which will be hidden by curved cards later on.

Cover the inside with cardstock. The cards are flush with the top without overlaps.

Cut a circle out of the top cardboard 13.8 cm diameter (keep the cutout). Cover the rim of the circle with a band of fabric 2 cm wide (it's much easier to use fabric rather than skivertex or paper) (1).

Glue the top to the box and reinforce it underneath with bands of Kraft.

Check the assembly cards and glue bands of Kraft to all the sides of two 0.7 mm cards (pink the rounded sides) and put them in place opposite each other (2 & 3).

Glue bands of Kraft to the two remaining cards and put them in place and then glue bands of fabric 2 cm wide onto the spines (4).

Cover the 0.7 mm cards; fold under the overlaps on the rounded sides. Glue them to each side; fold the overlaps over the top and under the bottom of the box.

Cover the base and glue it in place (5).

Cut a 0.7 mm card to cover the top (20.3 × 20.3 cm, to be checked in relation to your box). Cut out a circle 14 cm diameter, cover it, fold under the overlaps and glue it to the top of the box.

Here I did two cards: one is covered in fabric; the other, with the angles cut out, is covered in paper (5).

THE LID

Glue 2 round pieces of cardboard 14.4 cm in diameter, one on top of the other, and cover one side with fabric. Pink the overlaps and fold them underneath the circle. Cover a third round piece of cardboard with fabric or paper. Fold under the overlaps and glue the two pieces together, underside against underside. You can add piping around the seam if you like. Put a weight on it until dry.

Add a pretty button and the box is finished. My button is a cabochon covered in a weave of beads—my second passion—glued to a square button and screwed in (6).

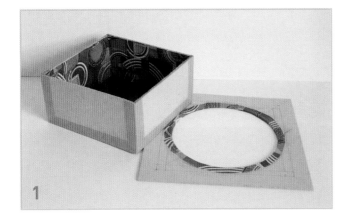

1

2

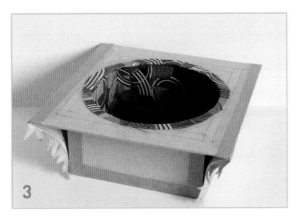

3

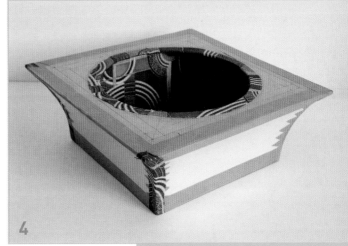

4

5

6

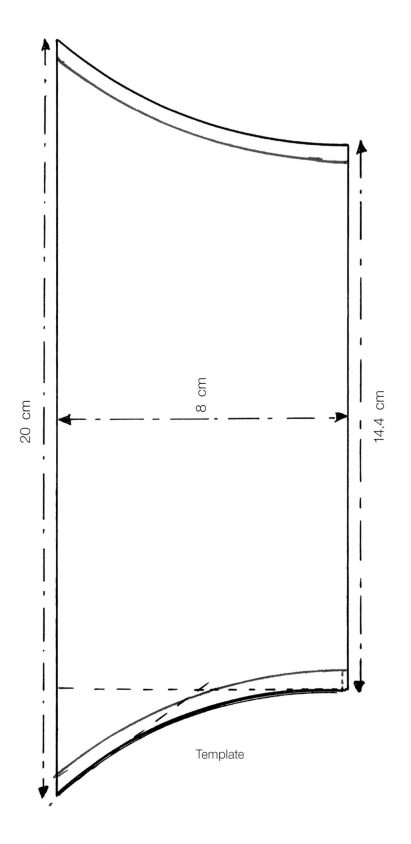

20 cm

8 cm

14.4 cm

Template

[Work basket]

The assembly of this basket is a little tricky, but the different shades of violet make it quite lovely.
You need to have two people to assemble this, so ask a friend to help you!
I made it as a work basket, but you can also make it in spring colors to use as you stroll in the garden.

MATERIALS
› Gray cardboard 2 mm
› Card 0.7 mm
› Cardstock
› Fabric
› Skivertex and paper
› Ribbon 70 x 30 cm
› 2 buttons

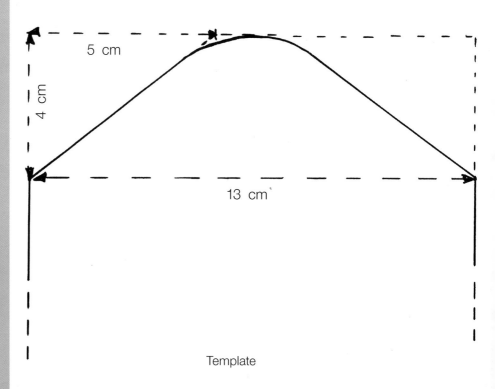

5 cm

4 cm

13 cm

Template

PROJECT

CUTTING OUT THE CARDBOARD

– Bottom: 28 × 16 cm
– Large sides: 28 × 10 cm (× 2)
– Small sides: 16 × 9.8 (× 2)
– Base: 28 × 16.8 cm
– Large sides, interior: 27.4 × 12 (× 2) to be checked
– Small sides, interior: 15.6 × 12 cm (× 2), to be checked
– Large supports for the compartment: 27 × 5.5 cm (× 2)
– Small supports for the compartment: 15.2 × 5.5 cm (× 2)
– Bottom of the compartment: 26.7 × 14.7 cm
– Large sides compartment: 26.7 × 6 cm (× 2)
– Small sides compartment: 14.7 × 5.8 cm (× 2)
– Partition compartment: 14.7 × 5.6c m (× 2)
– Small supports for lid compartments, left & right: 7 × 5 cm (× 4)
– Large supports for lid compartments, left & right: 14.1 × 5 cm (× 4)
– Small lid compartments, left & right: 14.5 × 7 cm (× 2)
– Uprights for the mini compartment in the center: 14.5 × 2.5 cm (× 2)
– Bottom of the mini compartment: 11 × 7.4 cm
– Large sides, mini compartment: 11 × 2.5 cm (× 2)
– Small sides, mini compartment: 7.4 × 2.3 cm (× 2)
– Bottom of the lid for the basket: 30.4 /28 × 3 cm
– Large sides, lid: 30.4/28 × 3 cm (× 2)
– Small sides, lid: 18.3/16.4 × 2.8 cm (× 2)

CUTTING OUT THE CARD

– Larges-side assembly: to be recut, each side, with the model 36 × 13 cm (× 2)
– Small-side assembly: to be recut, each side, with the model 24.5 × 13 cm (× 2)
– Large-side cover: 36.5 x 13.5 cm (× 2)
– Small-side cover: 25 x 13.5 cm (× 2)
– Interior of the handle: 80 × 4 cm
– Exterior of the handle: 60 × 4 cm

MAKING THE BOX

Make the box (see techniques on page 5).

Cut out the 0.7 mm assembly cards very carefully (pay attention to the direction of the card). You can slightly dampen the cards before assembling them to avoid breaking them.

Place bands of Kraft on all sides of the two 24.5 × 13 cm cards (pink at the rounded parts) and along the large sides of the two 36 × 13 cm cards. Place a small card on a large one, underside against underside, and fold the Kraft on the rounded side (1).

Place the other small card in the same way on the other side of the large card. To place the last card, you will need someone to keep the two sides to be joined curved. Glue the Kraft on one side and wait until it has completely dried before gluing the other side. Reinforce on the inside with bands of Kraft on the rounded sides.

Fit the box inside this assembly and fold the Kraft bands inside the box at the top and underneath at the bottom. You have finished the hard part! (2)

COVERING THE EXTERIOR OF THE BOX

Adjust the length of the small covering cards (25 × 13.5 cm) and cut out the rounded parts, following the model. Cover them with overlaps of 1.5 cm; glue them to each small side. Fold the overlaps all around, pinking the rounded parts (3).

Round off the 2 large covering cards. Cover them, fold under the overlaps on the rounded sides, and glue them to the box.

Fold the overlaps at the top inside the box and under the bottom. If the spines aren't perfect, you can always glue on some ribbons to hide them.

Cover the base, fold the overlaps, and glue it to the bottom of the box.

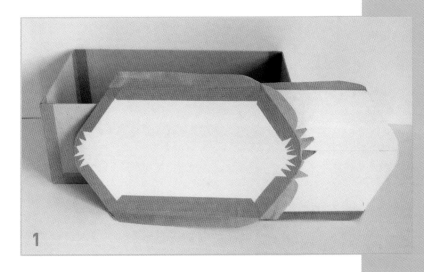

COVERING THE INTERIOR OF THE BOX

Cover the bottom with cardstock.

Cover the 2 cards for the handle, with overlaps only on the long sides. Fold the overlaps inward and glue the 2 together, underside against underside. The shorter one is on top and is only at the exterior of the box. You can eventually glue a ribbon to it. Glue the handle to the interior of the box, widening the bottom a little so that the lid, which is larger than the box, will fit properly (4).

Check the dimensions of the interior of the box before cutting out the cardboard interiors, they should go over the top of the box by 2 cm. Cover them with an overlap at the top of 3 cm and cut the angles according to Diagram 1.

Fold the side overlaps and then the bottom and the top ones. If you are using skivertex or paper, which is easier, you can cut it flush at the bottom.

Glue the large sides (4) and then the small sides (5).

Cut and adjust the compartment supports. Cover them in skivertex, with an overlap only at the top. Fold the overlap and glue the supports (6).

THE COMPARTMENT

I give the dimensions for the compartment, but it's better to calculate them according to your own box. Take the interior dimensions of your box (between the interior cardboards), so L is the length and W is the width of the box. The bottom of the compartment is calculated as follows:
– Length of the compartment = L – 0.3 cm
– Width of the compartment = W -0.7 cm

Take the height between the supports and the top of the box, H.
Height of the compartment = H–0.3 cm for the large sides and H – 0.5 cm for the small sides.

Make the compartment, cover the exterior of the 4 sides, and fold the overlaps into the top and under the bottom. Make a piece for the exterior bottom.

Cover the rim of the 2 partitions with a band of fabric 3 cm wide and position them with Kraft at 7 cm from each edge (make two small wedges to help you put them perfectly in place) (7).

THE LEFT AND RIGHT COMPARTMENTS

Make pieces for the bottoms. Create the sides with the cardboard that will serve as supports for the lids, which sit inside the compartments.

Cover the 4 sides, flush on 3 sides and with an overlap at the top. Fold in the overlap and glue 2 small sides opposite each other in the left and right compartments. Do the same for the large sides.

Check the lids and cover the top side, stitch on a button or ribbon, and cover the underside with cardstock (8 & 9).

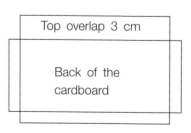

Diagram 1

4

5

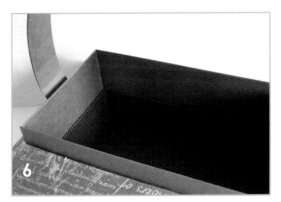

6

7

8

9

CENTER COMPARTMENT

Cover this compartment entirely in cardstock (see techniques on page 5) **(9)**.

I made a mini sling compartment inside. For this, cover the 2 uprights and glue them to the large sides. Make and cover the mini compartment **(10)**.

LID

The sides of the lid are slanting (Diagram 2). Make the lid. Use two pieces of cardstock for the small sides. Cover them, taking into account the interior sides so that you don't have to remake cards for the interior sides. Glue the cards to the small sides of the lid and fold the overlaps all around and inside, being careful with the slanting angles **(11)**.

Make 2 pieces for the large sides, cover them (the same as for the small sides), fold the 2 slanting small dies, and glue them to the large sides of the lid.

The top of the lid is made of 2 pieces of cardstock. The first is covered in pink paper, onto which I glued my decorations: 2 pieces of fabric and a transfer, under which I placed a thin piece of felting. The second is therefore open where the fabric and transfer are and is covered in violet paper. Open at 1 cm from the edges and fold the overlaps according to Diagram 3, shown below, which represents the underside of the card **(12)**.

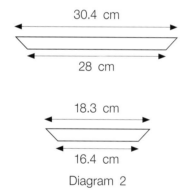

30.4 cm

28 cm

18.3 cm

16.4 cm

Diagram 2

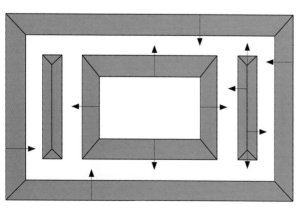

Diagram 3

10

11

12

[Makeup box]

A practical box for storing all your makeup. The 2 small rounded boxes in the front are open at the top for storing long brushes and cotton-wool balls. The extra: an interior mirror and lots of small draws for storing accessories and makeup.

MATERIALS
› Gray cardboard 2 mm
› Card 0.7 mm or cardboard 1 mm
› Cardstock
› Skivertex
› Fabric and 2 m of Liberty bias binding
› Mother-of-pearl beads
› 1 round mirror

PROJECT

CUTTING OUT THE CARDBOARD
Central box
– Bottom: 18 × 12 cm
– Large back and front: 18 × 12 cm (× 2)
– Small sides: 12 × 11.8 cm (× 2)
– Lid: 18.1 × 12.6 cm
– Bottom uprights: 17.5 × 1.6 cm (× 2)
– Bottom uprights: 11.6 × 1.6 cm (× 2)
– Floor: 17.5 × 12 cm
– Center side uprights: 8 × 1.6 cm (× 4)
– Sides: 12 × 8 cm (× 2)
– Ceiling: 17.5 × 12 cm
– Side uprights for the drawers: 3.7 × 12 cm (× 4)
– Bottom uprights: 3.7 × 13.4 cm (× 2)
– Shelf: 13.8 × 12 cm
– Bottoms, 2 drawers: 13 × 11.1 cm (× 2)
– Large sides, 2 drawers: 13.4 × 3.4 cm (× 4)
– Small sides, 2 drawers: 11.1 × 3.2 cm (× 2)
– Front, 2 drawers: 14 × 4 cm (× 2)

2 rectangular side boxes
– Bottoms (= back): 12 × 10 cm (× 2)
– Large sides: 12 × 10 cm (×4)
– Small sides: 10 × 9.8 cm (× 4)
– Uprights, large drawer sides: 7 × 9.7 cm (× 4)
– Uprights, bottom large drawer: 7 × 9.4 cm (× 2)
– Shelves: 9.8 × 9.7 cm (× 2)
– Uprights, small drawer sides: 4 × 9.7 cm (× 4)
– Uprights, bottom small drawer: 4 × 9.4 cm (× 2)
– Bottoms, 4 drawers: 9.1 × 8.2 cm (× 4)
– Large sides, 2 large drawers: 9.1 × 6.7 cm (× 4)
– Small sides, 2 large drawers: 8.2 × 6.5 cm (× 4)
– Large sides, 2 small drawers: 9.1 × 3.7 cm (× 4)
– Small sides, 2 small drawers: 8.2 × 3.5 cm (× 4)

2 rounded-sided boxes
– Back: 11.8 × 10 cm (× 2)
– 1 disc, diameter: 10 cm, cut in two

Finishing stage
– Bottom of the box to be cut out following the model: 39.6 × 16 cm
– Large back: 39.6 × 12.4 cm
– Small sides: 10 × 12.2 cm (× 2)
– Support, bottom of the box: 30 × 7 cm
– Large sides, support of the box: 30 × 4 cm (× 2)
– Small sides, support of the box: 7 × 3.8 cm (× 2)
– Base: 39.6 × 16 cm

Cutting out the 0.7 mm card (or 1 mm cardboard)
For the 2 round-sided boxes
– Assembly cards: 16 × 12 cm (× 2)
– Cover cards: 16.5 × 12 cm (× 2)

MAKING THE CENTRAL BOX
Make an opening in the front at 2 cm from the edges.

Make the box (see techniques on page 5).

Glue the 4 uprights that serve as support for the floor flush with the opening. Set the floor onto the supports and apply bands of Kraft to keep it in place.

Glue the side uprights and place the sides onto the uprights. Add bands of Kraft to keep them in place. Place the ceiling and add bands of Kraft. You should have a box that lies flush with the opening (1, 2 & 3).

COVERING THE CENTRAL BOX
Since my fabric was thin and light colored, I glued cardstock in the places I was gluing the fabric (see advice on page 10).

Cover the front exterior with an overlap of 3 cm at the top to cover the interior of the front of the upper compartment at the same time, and 3 cm for the sides, the box's sides being less deep. Fold back all the sides, and in the center make an opening 1.5 cm and fold back into the cavity.

Cover the sides of the upper partition with a piece of fabric 5 cm high so that you can cover the interior of the small sides at the same time.

Make a hinge with a band 7 cm high. Glue it to a reinforcement and place it so that it covers the interior back of the top partition.

Cut out 2 pieces of cardstock for the floor and the ceiling interiors of the central cavity. Cover them and fold under the overlaps before gluing them in place (4).

Check all the side, bottom, and shelf uprights and adjust them if necessary.

Cover them in skivertex: the side upright, flush on 3 sides with an overlap in front; the bottom upright, flush on all 4 sides, and the shelf is covered front on both upper and under side with one piece of skivertex (5).

Make and completely cover the 2 drawers.

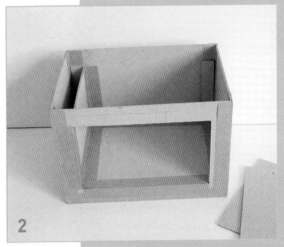

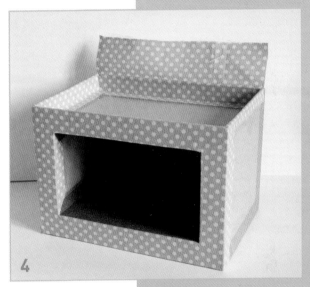

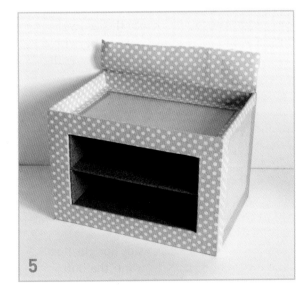

Check the front of the 2 drawers; cover them, folding back all the overlaps. If you have decided to add a ribbon, do so before gluing the front to the drawers; if not, you can simply screw on a button and glue the front onto the drawers (6).

Cut out a piece of cardstock for the bottom of the top compartment, cover it, fold under the overlaps, and glue it in place.

Cover the lid (see techniques on page 5: covering hinged lid). I covered mine in skivertex, with a 5 cm hinge at the back. And I made a smaller cardboard covered in fabric, with a button matching the ribbon to decorate it (7).

A small piece of advice: don't glue on your decorations right away; it will be more practical when gluing the boxes together and putting a weight on them.

PUTTING THE LID IN PLACE

Glue the exterior hinge first and leave it to dry properly before gluing the interior hinge (8 & 9).

Use cardstock for the interior of the lid; the mirror is just glued on (10).

MAKING AND COVERING THE RECTANGULAR SIDE BOXES

Make the 2 rectangular boxes (see techniques on page 5).

Covering the rectangular side boxes: cover the top with overlaps on all sides. Cover the edge of the bottom and one of the sides with bands 4 cm wide. Make an interior hinge on the other side (11). Be sure to reverse the hinges on the two boxes.

Cover the interior floor and ceiling with cardstock.

Cover the uprights for the shelf in the same way you did for the central box, and glue them in place.

Make and cover the two drawers on each side. I chose the same decorations as the front of the central drawers, but on a 0.7 mm card to limit the thickness (12).

MAKING AND COVERING THE ROUND-SIDED BOXES

Check the assembly so far and adjust it if necessary.

Assemble the back and the half circle. Glue bands of Kraft astride the 2 small sides and a large side of the assembly card (I used 1 mm cardboard) and place it in position (13).

Adjust the covering cards and glue them to the skivertex, with overlaps of 1.5 cm on 3 sides and 4 cm on a small side for the hinge. Glue the card to the box and fold in the 3 sides. Glue a small band of skivertex to the edge of the back and make a piece for under the box; the right overlap of this card is glued behind the box (14).

Use cardstock inside the two round-sided boxes and glue on ribbon or screw in a button.

Assemble the two round-sided boxes and the rectangular side boxes. For this, glue the exterior hinge first (15) and then the interior hinge (16).

Use cardstock for the back of the round-sided boxes.

Assemble the two boxes on each side of the central box. For this, glue the sides, aligning the backs, and leave to dry completely.

FINISHING TOUCHES

Check the dimensions of the surrounding box. Cut out the bottom, following Template 1 (or, even better, trace round your box and add 1 cm at the front), and assemble the box with the back and the small sides. Cover the sides and the bottom with a band of fabric 65 × 16 cm; fold in the overlaps on all sides. Cover the visible part of the bottom interior and fold the overlap underneath. Make a piece for the bottom exterior (17).

Glue the assembled boxes inside the surrounding box.

I chose to add a support to my makeup box, so that the mirror was at a better height for applying makeup and to give the box an airy look, but you don't have to—you can stop right there!

Make the support box and cover only the exterior. Round off the front corners of the support as in the photo and cover the top, folding the overlaps under on all sides. Use cardstock for underneath (18).

Glue the makeup box onto the support.

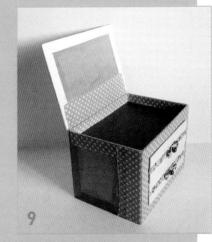

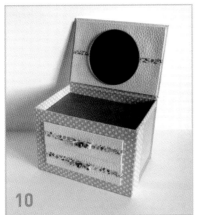

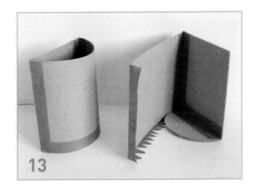

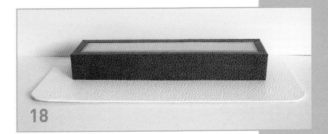

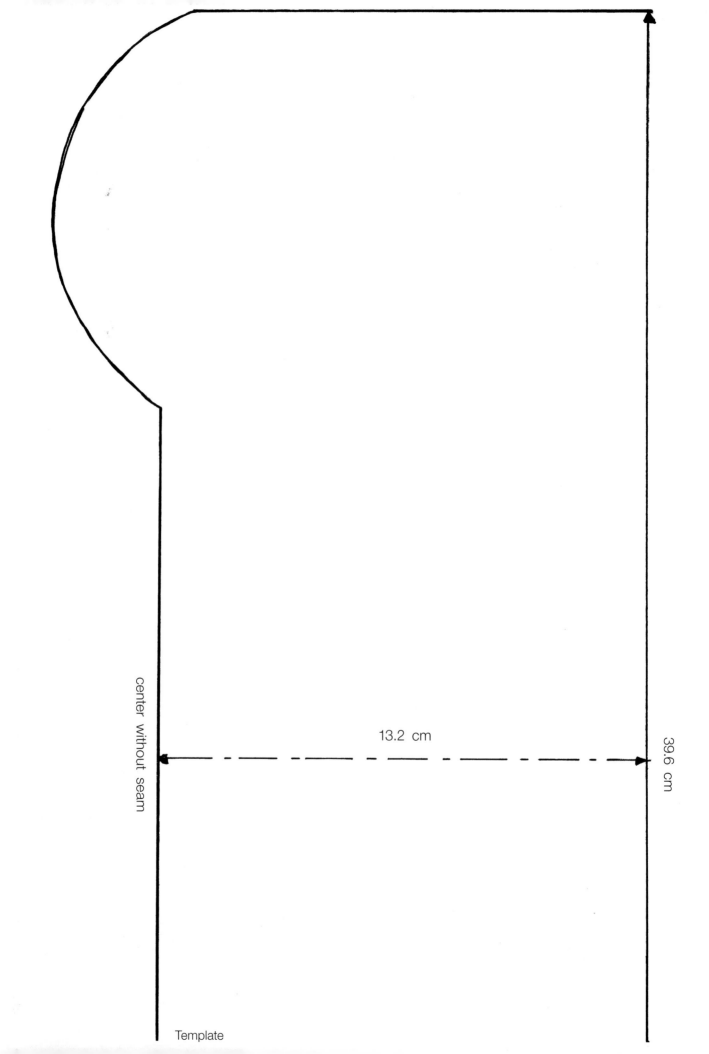

center without seam

13.2 cm

39.6 cm

Template

Acknowledgments

A huge thank-you to all my students for their encouragement throughout the year and for their enormous support during my illness.

Special thanks go to my friend Françoise, who, as usual, carefully reread my manuscript.

A heartfelt thank-you to my husband (I know that I'm not always easy to put up with while I'm creating things) and to my sons and grandson, who are the sunshine in my life.

If you would like to contact the author:

Blog: annebeads.blogspot.fr
Email: alardy.beads@gmail.com

Other Schiffer Books on Related Subjects:
The Great Book of Cardboard Furniture: Step-by-Step Techniques and Designs, Kiki Carton, ISBN 978-0-7643-4151-9

Upcycling Books: Decorative Objects, Julia Rubio, ISBN 978-0-7643-5875-3

Copyright © 2020 by Schiffer Publishing, Ltd.

Originally published as *Cartonnage Vintage* ©2016, L'Inédite, une marque des éditions Leduc.s, Paris, France
Translated from the French by Omicron Language Solutions, LLC

Library of Congress Control Number: 2019947655

Cover design: Molly Shields
Type set in DIN/Cambria
Editorial coordinator: Laurence Copsidas
Design concept: Géraud Lantuéjoul
Photos: Franck Schmitt
The materials shown in the photos were sourced from these retailers: L'Eclat de verre; La théière de bois; Perles & Co.; and Atilolou

ISBN: 978-0-7643-5965-1
Printed in China

Published by Schiffer Publishing, Ltd.
4880 Lower Valley Road
Atglen, PA 19310
Phone: (610) 593-1777; Fax: (610) 593-2002
E-mail: Info@schifferbooks.com
Web: www.schifferbooks.com

For our complete selection of fine books on this and related subjects, please visit our website at www.schifferbooks.com. You may also write for a free catalog.

Schiffer Publishing's titles are available at special discounts for bulk purchases for sales promotions or premiums. Special editions, including personalized covers, corporate imprints, and excerpts, can be created in large quantities for special needs. For more information, contact the publisher.

We are always looking for people to write books on new and related subjects. If you have an idea for a book, please contact us at proposals@schifferbooks.com.